BETWEEN THE FLAMES

Life as a Volunteer Firefighter

Maria D. Johnson

DEDICATION

This book is dedicated to my fellow firefighters, whose courage, dedication, and unwavering support have been a source of inspiration and strength. To my family and friends, thank you for your patience, understanding, and love. And to the reader, may you find inspiration and insight in these pages as you embark on your own journey, whatever it may be.

CONTENT

INTRODUCTION

My name is Bill Blackwell. I'm a volunteer firefighter for the Florence Township Fire Department in Florence Township, New Jersey. When I joined in 2006, the department was a combination of volunteers and career firefighters. Over the years, I've had some memorable experiences with all kinds of calls and emergencies. However, there is one battle I've always been in the middle of, and I don't think I'd ever choose a side in the conflict between career and volunteer firefighters.

Sure, I remember my roots and where I come from, but I am also reminded of who teaches me, wants me around, and takes care of me. Since 2016, when FTFD hired a few more career firefighters, I've seen and heard the drama that they received from the volunteers, and vice versa.

My struggle? The fear of having to pick a side while trying to make both sides work together for the same goal of protecting the lives and property of the residents in our community.

One of the reasons why I write a book about life as a volunteer fireman in a department that has both career and volunteer guys is that the public sees us as a group that does the coolest things in the world, like being the hero, riding cool trucks, and being the highlight of parades. But, out of the public eye, there's drama, betrayal, and political bull. Loyalty and leadership are questioned.

Ego gets in the way sometimes. There's always that guy who wants to be the John Wayne of the fire service. There's the guy who is just a name with a title and has no experience whatsoever. There's the cliques, the secrets, the truths, and everything in between.

What I'm about to start writing is a novel inspired by true events. No real names or stations will be used. If you feel like a character is about you, it's probably not, but if the bunker gear fits,.

I decided the best way to explain what it is like to be a volunteer in a career house is to put it in writing. I see the best and worst of both worlds.

1

↔

JOINING THE FIREHOUSE

My interest in firefighting and how I decided to become a volunteer

I'm a fifth generation volunteer firefighter. I didn't think I'd actually get to be one, but there I was, joining the firehouse I grew up in and going to the academy.

I remember watching them with awe as they raced past my house in their bright red trucks, sirens blaring, on their way to save lives and property. It wasn't just the thrill of the big red engines or the flashing lights; it was the idea of heroes in our midst, everyday people who risked everything to keep our community safe.

This early fascination planted a seed that would grow into a lifelong passion.

The Application and Training Process

I joined in 2006, tried EMT school but failed (never went back). Went to fire school in 2007 and got certified. Next came the physical agility test. This was perhaps the most daunting part of the application process. It involved a series of physically demanding tasks that simulated real-life firefighting scenarios: climbing ladders, carrying heavy equipment, dragging a dummy to safety, and navigating through confined spaces. I trained intensively, focusing on building my strength, stamina, and endurance. The day of the test, I pushed myself to my limits and beyond. When I finally crossed the finish line, drenched in sweat but triumphant, I knew I had given it my all.

After passing the physical agility test, I underwent a series of interviews with the fire department's officers. These interviews were designed to assess my character, commitment, and compatibility with the team. I spoke candidly about my motivations, my respect for the profession, and my eagerness to contribute to the community. I felt a deep sense of alignment with the values and mission of the fire department, and I hoped they could see my genuine passion.

The final step was a background check and medical examination. The fire department needed to ensure that I was not only physically fit but also of sound mind and character. I passed these checks without issue, and at long last, I received the official notification: I had been accepted as a volunteer firefighter. I've been volunteering ever since then.

My first day at the firehouse and initial interactions with career firefighters

I don't exactly remember my first day. I joined in 2006 when the firehouse was mainly volunteer with few career staff. Over the years, more guys got hired, and volunteers would stop coming around. I soon grew closer with the career guys, more than I was with three volunteers.

The night before my first shift, I could hardly sleep. A mix of excitement and nerves kept me awake, imagining what lay ahead. As I walked through the doors of the firehouse for the first time, I was met with a barrage of sights, sounds, and smells that would soon become familiar. The gleaming fire trucks, the distant hum of radios, the faint scent of smoke and gear – it was both overwhelming and exhilarating.

I was introduced to the team, a group of seasoned career firefighters whose expressions ranged from curious to skeptical. I could sense the unspoken questions: Would this volunteer be up to the task? Could I earn their respect and trust? I knew I had a lot to prove. My first shift was a whirlwind of orientation and introductions.

2

↔

GAINING ACCEPTANCE

Proving My Worth

Earning a place in the firehouse as a volunteer was a continuous process that required proving my worth on every call and during every training session. The career firefighters had a high standard, and rightly so—their lives and the lives of others depended on it. My journey to gain their acceptance was marked by key moments where I demonstrated my skills and dedication.

One such moment occurred during a particularly harrowing house fire. It was a call that came in the middle of a sweltering summer afternoon. A two-story home was engulfed in flames, and we knew there were people trapped inside. As we arrived on the scene, the intensity of the situation was immediately apparent.

Captain Flyer quickly assigned roles. I was tasked with supporting the hose line team, ensuring the water supply remained steady. As the team advanced into the burning house, the heat was overwhelming. Sweat poured down my face, mixing with the soot and grime.

Suddenly, there was a shout from inside the house. One of the firefighters, Estelow, had gotten separated from the team and was in trouble. Without hesitation, I grabbed an extra hose and moved towards the sound, coordinating with Captain Flyer through my radio. The heat was intense, but I pushed forward, focused on finding Estelow.

I found him near a collapsing wall, struggling to stay upright. Together, we managed to navigate back to the exit, the flames closing in around us. It was a close call, but we made it out safely. As we regrouped outside, the other firefighters gave me nods of acknowledgment.

Estelow clapped me on the shoulder, his expression a mix of gratitude and respect. It was at that moment I felt a significant shift in how I was perceived by my peers.

Building Relationships

Developing friendships and bonds with career firefighters was crucial to integrating into the firehouse community. Over time, I found myself becoming more involved in their world, both professionally and personally. It was through these relationships that I began to feel like a true member of the team.

One of the most impactful relationships I built was with Lieutenant Harris. Known for his tough exterior and no-nonsense approach, he was initially one of the hardest to impress. But as we worked together on various calls, I started to see another side of him—a side that deeply cared about the team and their well-being.

During downtime, Harris and I would often find ourselves talking about firefighting techniques, strategies, and the experiences that had shaped our lives. He began to share stories from his early days, mistakes he had made, and lessons he had learned. These conversations were invaluable, providing me with insights that textbooks and training sessions could never offer.

One evening, after a particularly exhausting day, Harris invited me to join him and a few others for a drink at a local bar. It was a simple gesture, but it marked a turning point. Sitting there, sharing stories and laughter, I realized I was no longer just a volunteer in their eyes—I was part of the team.

Teamwork and Mutual Support

The firehouse operated on a foundation of teamwork and mutual support. Every call and every training session were a testament to the importance of working together. I quickly learned that my success depended on my ability to function as part of this cohesive unit.

During a large-scale training exercise, we simulated a high-rise building fire. The scenario was designed to test our coordination and response times under pressure. I was paired with Todd, a career firefighter who was known for her meticulous approach to firefighting.

As we navigated through the mock building, communicating through our radios and coordinating our movements, I felt a sense of synchronicity. We operated as a single entity, with each move calculated and purposeful. By the end of the exercise, we had successfully completed our objectives, and our teamwork was praised by the instructors.

Todd turned to me after the exercise, a rare smile on his face. "You did good out there," he said. "We made a solid team." His words reinforced the importance of trust and collaboration. It wasn't just about individual skills; it was about how well we could work together when it mattered most.

3

↔

THE BROTHERHOOD OF FIREFIGHTERS

Shared Experiences

The bond among firefighters is forged in the crucible of shared experiences. The firehouse is more than just a place of work; it's a second home where we face dangers together, celebrate victories, and support each other through the hardest times. Over time, these shared experiences created a sense of brotherhood that transcended the career-volunteer divide.

One of the most poignant examples of this bond occurred during a massive industrial fire. The blaze had spread rapidly through a factory, threatening nearby buildings and lives. When we arrived on the scene, the heat was intense, and the air was thick with smoke and the acrid smell of burning chemicals.

We worked tirelessly for hours, battling the flames and ensuring that everyone was evacuated safely. At one point, we were inside the factory, trying to control a particularly stubborn fire. The structure groaned ominously, and I could see the worry etched on the faces of my fellow firefighters.

In the midst of the chaos, I found myself next to Estelow, a career firefighter who had initially been one of my toughest critics. As we maneuvered the hose, the ceiling above us began to collapse. Without a moment's hesitation, Estelow pushed me out of the way, taking the brunt of the debris himself. We managed to pull him out and get him to safety, but it was a close call.

Back at the firehouse, as we debriefed and checked on Estelow, the reality of what had happened sank in. Estelow's actions saved my life. It was a stark reminder of the risks we faced and the depth of the bond that had formed between us. In that moment, I realized that we were more than just colleagues—we were brothers and sisters, united by our commitment to protect and serve.

Emotional Highs and Lows

Firefighting is a rollercoaster of emotions. The highs are exhilarating, but the lows can be devastating. These emotional extremes are part of what binds us together, creating a deep sense of empathy and understanding among firefighters.

One of the most significant highs I experienced was during a residential fire rescue operation. We received a call about a house engulfed in flames, with reports of a child trapped inside. The urgency of the situation hit us all hard. As we arrived, we could see the frantic parents outside, their faces etched with fear and desperation.

I was part of the search and rescue team that entered the house. The smoke was thick, and visibility was almost zero. We moved methodically, calling out and listening for any signs of life. Finally, we heard a faint cry from the back room. Pushing through the smoke and heat, we found the child huddled in a corner, terrified but alive.

Carrying the child out and handing him over to his parents was one of the most rewarding moments of my life. The relief and gratitude in their eyes were overwhelming. Back at the firehouse, we celebrated the successful rescue and the high of saving a life, fueling our spirits.

But with the highs come the inevitable lows. Not every call ends with a happy outcome. There was one time we responded to a multi-vehicle accident on a rain-slicked highway. Despite our best efforts, we couldn't save everyone. The grief and frustration were palpable as we returned to the firehouse, the weight of the loss heavy on our shoulders.

In those moments, the support of my fellow firefighters was crucial. We leaned on each other, shared our pain, and found ways to cope together. It was through these emotional lows that I truly understood the depth of the brotherhood among us. We were each other's lifeline, helping each other navigate the darkest times.

Looking Out for Each Other

The ethos of looking out for each other is deeply ingrained in the culture of the firehouse. It goes beyond professional responsibility; it's about personal commitment and care for one another's well-being. As a volunteer working with career firefighters, I experienced this support in profound ways.

One evening, after a particularly grueling day, I was visibly exhausted and struggling to keep up. Lieutenant Harris pulled me aside. "You need to take care of yourself," he said, his tone firm but caring. "If you're not at your best, you can't help anyone else." His advice was a reminder of the importance of self-care, a lesson that was reinforced by the actions of my peers.

During another intense training session, I injured my ankle. It wasn't a severe injury, but it was enough to slow me down. The career firefighters didn't hesitate. They took over my tasks, ensuring that I could rest and recover. Their actions were a testament to the sense of family within the firehouse. It wasn't just about completing the job; it was about ensuring that every member of the team was taken care of.

The assistance extended beyond physical well-being. There were times when the emotional toll of the job weighed heavily on me. After a particularly traumatic call where we lost a young life, I found it hard to shake off the grief. Todd, who had become a close friend, noticed my struggle. He sat with me, offering a listening ear and words of comfort. His presence was a lifeline, helping me process the pain and find a way to move forward.

4

↔

THE CHALLENGES

Balancing Volunteer Work and Personal Life

Being a volunteer firefighter in a career firehouse demanded a level of commitment and sacrifice that often blurred the lines between duty and personal life. Juggling multiple responsibilities—work, family, and the firehouse—was a constant challenge, requiring careful time management and a supportive network.

Early mornings often started with my regular job, followed by afternoons and nights at the firehouse. The physical and emotional demands were relentless. There were days when I'd barely have time to catch my breath between responsibilities, let alone spend quality time with family and friends. The strain was real, and maintaining balance was an ongoing struggle.

One particularly challenging period was when a series of major fires broke out in quick succession. For nearly a week, I was at the firehouse almost non-stop, returning home only to shower and grab a few hours of sleep. My family missed me, and I missed them. The separation was hard, especially for my partner, who had to handle everything at home alone.

During one of the rare moments I was home, my partner sat me down. "We need you here too," they said, their voice filled with concern. "The firehouse is important, but so are we." Their words hit home. I realized I needed to find a better way to balance my dual roles. I started scheduling regular family time, ensuring that I was present for important events and moments.

Communication became key. I kept my family informed about my schedule and the firehouse's demands. At the same time, I shared my home responsibilities with my colleagues, who were surprisingly understanding and supportive. They covered for me when needed, allowing me to maintain a healthier balance.

Managing Stress and Burnout

Firefighting is inherently stressful. The constant state of readiness, the adrenaline rush during emergencies, and the emotional toll of witnessing traumatic events can lead to burnout if not managed properly. As a volunteer, the challenge was even greater because I had to switch between different roles and responsibilities on a daily basis.

I quickly learned the importance of stress management techniques. Physical fitness played a crucial role. Regular exercise helped me maintain the stamina needed for the job and also served as an outlet for stress. Running, weightlifting, and yoga became essential parts of my routine.

Mentally, I found solace in mindfulness practices. Meditation and deep-breathing exercises helped me stay centered, especially after particularly tough calls. It was a way to decompress and reset, ensuring that I didn't carry the weight of one emergency into the next.

Support from my fellow firefighters was another vital component. We had an unspoken agreement to check in on each other, especially after difficult calls. Sometimes, it was as simple as a shared cup of coffee and a chat. Other times, it involved more formal debriefs where we could talk openly about our experiences and emotions.

One of the lowest points for me was after a particularly traumatic call involving a child. The memory haunted me, affecting my sleep and my mood. Recognizing the signs of burnout, I sought help from a counselor who specialized in trauma. The sessions were immensely helpful, providing me with tools to process the experience and cope with the ongoing demands of firefighting.

Navigating Conflicts

Even if they were difficult, conflicts provided possibilities for personal development and education. In order to successfully navigate them, you needed to demonstrate diplomacy, patience, and a willingness to view things from a variety of angles.

The distribution of resources was a significant cause of contention. As a result of a lack of available equipment during a particularly busy season, emotions increased around who should be given priority. Due to the fact that they are professionals who work full-time, career firemen believed that they should be given priority admission. It was maintained by the volunteers that in order to be effective, they need sufficient resources.

A debate that was mediated and during which all parties had the opportunity to submit their arguments led to the resolution. We were able to come to an agreement that prioritized resources according to the level of urgency of the calls and the number of workers that were available. Despite the fact that it was not an ideal answer, it served as evidence that we were able to discover solutions that were feasible via effective communication and collaboration.

5

↔

THE LEARNING CURVE

Mastering Techniques and Skills

My decision to become a volunteer at a career firehouse meant that I needed to quickly become proficient in a wide variety of technical skills and methods. The professional firemen were specialists, and to win their respect, I needed to be skilled in every part of the job. This stage of my journey was all about learning, growing, and proving myself via action.

Donning and doffing were the first skills I concentrated on. Things involve placing things appropriately in a timely and effective manner. Donning and doffing are what protects us from the smoke-filled surroundings. My early attempts were sloppy, and I struggled to wield the heavy hose while communicating with my crew.

Andrew, the same professional firefighter who had previously criticized my attempts, took me under his wing. He spent hours with me after shifts, demonstrating strategies to increase my grip, posture, and coordination. His patience and devotion were important. Slowly, I began to observe progress. During a particularly tough practice, I managed to handle the hose properly, gaining a nod of appreciation from Andrew and others. It was a modest win, but it meant the world to me.

Specialized Training and Certification

Beyond the basics, there were specialized skills and certifications that I needed to acquire. Each certification not only enhanced my capabilities but also increased my credibility among career firefighters. One of the first certifications I pursued was Firefighter 1 and Vehicle Extrication 1. I got Emergency Medical Responder and Firefighter 2 certifications this year. The training was intense, covering everything from chemical identification to decontamination procedures.

The classroom sessions were grueling, filled with complex information and technical jargon. But the hands-on exercises were even more demanding. We practiced donning and doffing protective suits, handling hazardous spills, and coordinating with other emergency services. It was during these practical sessions that I truly understood the importance of precision and calm under pressure.

During my EMT training, one memorable experience was assisting in a high-stakes rescue. We responded to a severe car accident, and I found myself performing CPR on a critically injured passenger. The training kicked in instinctively, and we managed to stabilize the patient until we reached the hospital. The experience was both harrowing and exhilarating, reinforcing the importance of being well-prepared.

Learning from Mistakes

Making mistakes was unavoidable, particularly in a situation with such high stakes. Every error served as a teaching moment, frequently more beneficial than any official instruction. When a regular fire practice went awry, I learned something of the utmost importance.

My responsibility was to oversee a group of people doing a search and rescue during our multi-story building fire simulation. I made a bad decision during the practice, leading my squad to a stairway that was meant to be clear but had been designated as dangerous. In a true scenario, the error may have been devastating and resulted in a delay.

Following the training, Captain Flyer convened the crew for a debriefing. He spoke candidly. "Errors such as those can result in fatalities," he stated firmly. Although it was difficult to hear, his criticism was essential. I paid close attention to what he said, researching building plans and honing my decision-making techniques. The event made me a more careful and cautious fireman.

An even minor, but equally significant, error taught us another lesson. I misused a piece of equipment during a night shift, which resulted in a coworker suffering a minor injury. The remorse set in quickly and deeply. I accepted full responsibility and apologized. Estelow, the hurt firefighter, comforted me by saying, "Mistakes are made by everyone. It's critical that we take what we've learned from them and move forward. His pardon and encouragement were invaluable in enabling me to progress and get well.

Mentorship and Guidance

The coaching and advice I got were priceless along this learning curve. The professional firefighters, who had previously been uneasy about me, became my guides and instructors. Their expertise and readiness to impart it to me were really helpful to my development.

Among them, Lieutenant Harris was particularly important. He frequently spent time going over the finer details of tactics and strategies used in combating fires. We spoke about various situations for hours on end, reviewed previous calls, and made plans for upcoming difficulties. His guidance went beyond only imparting technical knowledge; he also imparted leadership qualities, resilience, and the value of maintaining composure under duress.

Todd also became a friend and mentor. He held himself and everyone else to the highest standards and was extremely careful in his approach to combating fires. He gave candid, although usually helpful, criticism. He challenged me to always strive for perfection, to think critically, and to be a better person.

With their aid, I was able to become a better firefighter and further integrate into the firehouse community. Their ability to make me feel appreciated and cherished gave me more self-assurance and inspired me to never stop trying to do better.

CONCLUSION

↔

REFLECTING ON THE JOURNEY

Personal Growth and Transformation

It's amazing to see the change when I reflect on my time spent as a volunteer fireman at a career station. I didn't know where I fit in or what I was capable of at first. With perseverance, diligence, and the steadfast support of my fellow firefighters, I developed into a capable and well-respected team member over time. This trip was about more than simply credentials and skill mastery; it was about resilience, personal growth, and the strong ties formed in the furnace of shared experiences.

The difficulties I encountered—managing stress and burnout, resolving disagreements, and juggling my personal life with the responsibilities of volunteering—were all part of a greater journey of self-discovery and growth. Every challenge conquered, every lesson discovered, and every instance of friendship shaped the person I am today.

The Value of Brotherhood and Teamwork

One of the most profound lessons I learned was the value of brotherhood and teamwork. The firehouse was more than just a place of work; it was a family home. The bonds I formed with my fellow firefighters were based on trust, respect, and mutual support. These relationships were crucial, providing the foundation upon which our effectiveness and safety depended.

The shared experiences, from the highs of successful rescues to the lows of tragic losses, created a sense of unity that transcended individual differences. Whether career or volunteer, we were all part of the same team, working towards a common goal. This sense of brotherhood was a constant source of strength, motivation, and comfort.

The ongoing journey

While this book captures a significant chapter of my life, the journey is far from over. The lessons learned and the bonds formed continue to shape my path as a firefighter and beyond. The firehouse remains a place of continuous learning, challenges, and growth. Every call, every training session, and every interaction with my peers adds to the rich tapestry of my experience.

Looking ahead, I am committed to giving back to the firehouse community that has given me so much. Mentoring new volunteers, sharing my experiences, and continuing to improve my skills are ways I can contribute. The fire service is a lifelong journey, and I am proud to be part of this dedicated and courageous community.

Final Reflections

Reflecting on this journey, I am filled with a deep sense of gratitude. I am grateful for the opportunity to serve, for the support of my family and friends, and for the mentorship and camaraderie of my fellow firefighters. This experience has taught me invaluable lessons about resilience, teamwork, and the importance of community.

To anyone considering becoming a volunteer firefighter, I offer this: It is a path filled with challenges, but it is also one of the most rewarding and transformative experiences you can undertake. The skills you acquire, the bonds you form, and the personal growth you achieve are unparalleled.

In conclusion, my time as a volunteer firefighter in a career firehouse has been a journey of growth, learning, and profound connection. It has shaped me in ways I could never have imagined, and for that, I am forever grateful. The fire service is a unique and noble calling, and I am honored to be part of this extraordinary brotherhood.